# YOU ARE NOT WHO YOU CLAIM

# YOU
# ARE NOT
# WHO YOU
# CLAIM

## Evelyn Lau

**Porcépic Books**
Victoria

This edition is published by Press Porcépic Limited, 4252 Com-
merce Circle, Victoria, B.C. V8Z 4M2, with the assistance of the
Canada Council.

**Canadian Cataloguing in Publication Data**

Lau, Evelyn, 1971-
    You are not who you claim


    Poems.  ISBN  0-88878-291-8
I. Title. PS8573.A92Y6 1990   C811'.54    C90-091265-0
PR9199.3.L38Y6 1990

This book is dedicated to the people I met
who tried so hard to be people they could admire,
and in their failures inspired many of these poems.

# ROLE MODELS

We've all had one, seen him fall
I want now
to take thumb and forefinger, pinch my ears shut
against the sound of your words, panes of glass
shattering in the sink
your laughter like a kitten
licking itself dead in a corner somewhere
you may bury it here, like this, in the wide space
my arms have opened for you

You arrive on my doorstep
I seem a small thing to sacrifice
we rise out of the city and the sun
fingers down through the branches
you watch teenage girls cross the road, your eyes
weave stockings to fit their legs
they carry their breasts like welcome burdens
your daughter stands in a doorway and you hunger
for her, the body she must have stolen
while your back was turned

You point me to the night, the white pennies
of streetlamps barricading the sky
you insist you are my savior
how can I help but know the truth
and love you for your lies

A voice like a tranquilizer
drops onto my tongue from the phone
there's nothing to say but I see you still
elbow propped on your briefcase
quick journalist eyes flashing
the promises in the car before good-bye, I didn't know then
that nobody who makes promises remembers them, I left
treasuring the handful of words
the hug being such a hard thing, bodies looping in seatbelts
kisses are tidier, no one thinks of cheeks as private places
mouths are dangerous and then disappointing

You stay one step ahead, walk lightly on weathered feet
I hear that I am vulnerable
you tell me things I never knew
the phone is forgotten against your ear, it crashes
into my hand
my heart beats like a pebble skipping water

You could have been successful at anything
why did it have to be manipulation

## LAWYERS

Pens pinched between buffed nails,
sausage fingers bending,
lawyers denude the page
pulling out strings of obscure sentences.
My eyes orbit the office, stationed above
a dime-circle sun, concrete, the city a medley of grey
thru slatted blinds

    In my dreams there is no time for
    negotiations, policies, fees--
    I stand in broken alleys, am swept to sleep
    by blowing rain and garbage.
    Hands slapping tongues of fire,
    I beat at the flames.

Their faces change each day, by God and yet
that flick of the pen similarly elegant;
they wear gold pens in their pockets and pink flowers for noses
as if from embarrassment or cold . . .
Their eyes are water pebbles, earth stones,
steel.
Like fat angels, they hum
in the lobby afterwards, beckoning elevators with
eyes molten as melted money

    In my dreams I stand honorably
    in the corridors of the street, the rain
    soft sucking in a vacuum.
    I refuse the original seduction of fire
    blazing beasts into civilization--
    O in my dreams I resist premeditated applause,
    I slide down rainswept streets where
    fantasies clothe me splendidly enough.

## LITERARY LION

I watch your legs conquer the distance
between audience and stage
you wear neon and leather like badges
I cannot see through fluorescent colors, I can't
hear past your jokes, hard slaps into the microphone
no one needed you to be tough but you got that way
as though summoned
the lines in your face spectacular victories

You expand under the stage light, timing perfect
we turn our faces up like flowers
waiting to be picked
you pause, flick your eyes
enjoy the tears you provoke
who says men can't be seductive?
I think you are smiling at me
or someone behind my right shoulder

Listening, I feel again your weight on the bed
springs obeying laws of gravity
you told secrets which could have been lies
I believed not enough in those days, nor now
maybe it's safer or maybe it's the losses I like
distances to grieve over, good-byes to tie up in blue ribbons
like old love letters

There is such hard pain in you
it almost justifies the behavior
you walk off the stage into people's arms
the words are small now and quiet
you crush pens like blossoms in your hands, sign autographs
the women treasure, you instantly forget
I wait only seconds before leaving
it takes only seconds to say good-bye

# AN AFTERNOON CAPPUCCINO

if each intensity of emotion is an addiction
you should have stayed in that basement
circled by bags of powder, razors, glassy eyes
the one window opaque with grime

but you got up and got away.
Now you sprawl, legs open
in a cafe doorway in the west end
shirt deliberately unbuttoned, a showcase
of chest hair gleaming gold

You harden your muscles into ridges.
Smug under a spotlight of sun,
your eyes pull at passing women
tongue flicking at foam from a cappuccino

Just coz you care doesn't mean you're addicted,
I want to say:
Just coz you're in love doesn't mean you got to
run away--
but you lid your pale eyes, flash them
sleazy white fire
at women in heels, decaying
behind colored contacts and stiff stuck mascara

I sit here stirring this insipid coffee
with its soggy foam that just
disappears

your eyes seduce every woman, tongue
lingers wetly on a plastic spoon--
throned on a shiny pink chair,
foam curls your lips,
your scornful eyes snatch and dispose

coz if you don't care there's no addiction
and you don't want to be addicted again;
if it's one day at a time, you don't have to explain
licking the cloud of foam away
inviting the next pair of tight jeans over
for an afternoon cappucccino

## PSYCHIATRIST

and this, it has opened a wound in me

your face, stricken by fluorescent light
pores gaping
moisture squeezed from your forehead.
you unknot the secrets of your silk tie and
I breathe in sloped shoulders
a mountain of belly

    she rocks in a cradle of books
    bottles of wine

in the doorway you meet my editor
she slaps you with her eyes
your face is mute
as if too many warnings have crowded there
and died on your cheeks

    her eyes glow like pears
    arranged under lamps

sick sharp yellow
pinches your face
your voice leaps
finds no escape in walls, fractured tubes,
ceilings, heat shouting

    we laugh about you over wine
    unlocking secrets
    examining the contents of boxes of intimacies
    --you hold no magic here--
    her eyes approving each betrayal,
    I strut eagerly across magenta rug
    towards the blade of her pen
    open boxes in outstretched hands

It is you now, ungraced by softness
it is you abandoned
you sit full in my hands
you move alone across a beach in winter
like a child
like flesh in my cupped hands

    the editor, framed by plants and posters and thick color
    Indians in lotus position on the walls.
    I surrender to lamplight and laughter
    to winking glass, her smile birthing
    on wine-stained lips
    in a pool of paper
    and baubles and books and ponderous curtains

The hours of your sacrifice forgotten,
I hurry you into sky and trees
empty evening
You have no belonging here, and the door
staggers shut against your untouched face

## DRUGGED

Drugged, his mouth froze above her
a slice in a Hallowe'en pumpkin
drooling blue light.
She pulled out from under the twitching of his arms and legs
spiralling to the floor
hands outstretched for clothes tangled in the shadows.

A week ago
she had swayed up from the same bed
a bottle of vodka
a confusion of empty prescription bottles
naked on the dresser.
Over the sink, crescents of her face photographed
by stainless steel taps
as color jetted from her lips and swirled
down the drain.
She wandered into the hallway
groping in the flickering light, the mess
for the phone.
The darkness flashed,
ambulance lights spun her body
down
onto white sheets.
Faces swam under winter fluorescents
as she tugged at a snake they forced down her throat
into her stomach.
Then nothing
till the next day when, waking,
she found herself smudged with charcoal and blood.
Watching a red trickle
creep down her arm
she saw tubes glued to her veins.

Her pupils had long ago fled, in a pair,
from the bathroom mirror.
She slashed the eye-pencil under
the remaining glazed circles
noticing her fingers trembled when suspended in air.
The door, the hallway, then the basement dissolved:
he stood across the room
a pill between thumb and forefinger.
Her hands stretched out
to fill the void.

## FAREWELL TO A COMMERCIAL WRITER

used to be
your words sank like summer berries onto my tongue
each day now
I dream myself awake, rub raw the dark
till it bleeds into my facecloth
I peel loose the skins of drunkenness

mornings and sour wine taste the same
the distance dilates between us
words being useless vehicles of seduction,
I summon tears like flowers
they drink in the rain of your contempt

dawn struggles through the window
your eyes are innocent in that light
too bad the light changes so quickly

# THE ABYSS LOOKS BACK

3 AM rain, the sun squeezes its muscles shut against us
the short contractions of the heart
this is the hour people discover themselves in,
paralyzed by the Medusas they see
I doubt the sun will rise again:
you have torn a necklace of pearls between tense fingers
let them drop on pavement and grass

I draw the rain across my face
sit quiet, smoke cigarettes in a pale dome
wait for the silver chains to be hauled back into the sky
I must break that black umbrella
pull a crow's wing and a wire down your cheekbone
they say revenge is sweet, look for the tongue travelling the lips
the bright blindness when I raise my lids

## CRAVINGS

Dark faces crouch in the attic
with sun-staggered eyes.
She shrinks, foetal,
between cupboard and wall.

"I am dissolving out the window,
needy arms windmilling
into the blue of your eyes
blue
as ocean, sky and newborn babies.
Let me live in your cancer
and marry your pain."

(His eyes look up
cut, bleeding.
Broken blue prisms
lie sharp in her palm.)

She sacrificed pieces of her body
for a fantasy of warmth.
Now she flails
trapped in a ring of dark faces.

"Rub me in the ashes of your cigarettes,
Grind me into beer bottle shards,
Smear blood between my legs and watch it
swell
into rivers streaming down my thighs"

(He doesn't know how to hold her
broken yet trusting--
he watches as dark faces
wrestle her to the ground.)

"Don't leave me.
  Your fingers spring knives inside me.
  Let me eat your oyster mouth,
  your open cysts
  erupting juices down my chin.
  Shoot fear into the vein of my arm
  and watch it drip sweat from my fingers
  lash my breasts to shreads with your cock--
  Just don't leave me."

  (He smiles bitterly--
  dark faces lunge at her body.
  Two blue stones
  drop from her hand.)

"Andrew, let me suck the cancer out
 with my ardent teeth"

### THE QUIET ROOM

PSYCHIATRIC ASSESSMENT UNIT
VANCOUVER GENERAL HOSPITAL.


Naked feet
flop over the edge of the mattress
in Quiet Room #4.

The silence is a dead creature
stirring decay into the air conditioning
disguised by water dripping from a tap
a roll of toilet paper unbalancing from the toilet rim
scuttling across the floor,
noises swarming like flies over a carcass.

The observation camera blinks
at the flower of blood wilting on the ground
puckered as an old woman's lips,
the signature of a nurse stealing life
through a hole in the patient's arm.

Her dreams unfold now, in the air:
knives licking doctors' throats
dynamite to fragment the brick walls:
the cold barrels, their fear!
mirrored back into her eyes.

The observation camera swivels its attention
to the next patient:
his screaming.

# WRITERS

I never wanted it this way:
into my hands you've tossed unrevised dreams,
flabby folds of paper, edges pricking my palm.
No cosmetic's skilled enough to soften
the words snapped apart, bent
into bitter black letters

How I want this to stop:
this pilot light in the brain,
it never shuts off.
It sputters between our bodies.
I walk circles around your manuscripts,
shuffle a path through books bricking the walls,
cockroaches cracking underfoot,
filing cabinets vomiting dust.
I sweep your floor with my stockings

I wanted something more than this:
words leaping in claustrophobic apartments,
words standing like tears in your eyes.
Our flesh is dismembered by language,
pinched by wiry letters;
Words tense the muscles of the air,
words dine on the couch, spitting out foam,
timid strands of hair I pluck off my shirt each morning

No amount of whiteout can erase
the pain indelible in your eyes,
the imprint of typewriter keys checkering your face
(you passed out over the fifth draft
of your unpublished autobiography).
Your migraines command a fleet of shooting stars:
"They start in my eyeballs
They travel outwards in streaks of light--
Their fall is mesmerizing, but then they
burn out"

## IN RETROSPECT

waiting in the downtown confusion
I saw you standing, a reflection in a jewellry store window
bright muscles and snakeskin boots
jaw clenched in stubborn pain
eyes hidden behind a gust of wind

we made no promises, except one
which you broke
your letter comes six months too late
the days have stopped at the wrong station
there are no more trains

for the first time
I understand that hate in your eyes
I too have nothing harmless to offer
in retrospect, I wouldn't have touched you
I would have stayed home the day we met

## TALKING BACK

your wild eyes shifting about the office
drive at a lie which breaks the silence
I should have requested a Beethoven deafness at birth
to protect my art
to defeat your hurting words

my puzzled innocence is a turn-on
a challenge for the likes of you
your grabbing hands slam up against me
I applaud your display of power
I wear your pale exploitation without reproach
I could list each of your lies but
you are the master of this game
you dictate the roles of victim and abuser

I see that my efforts at decency meant nothing
reputations are dependent upon other people
their needs and their inadequacies
in my imagination I've already moved to a different city
changed my name
taken a nine to five job

you forget that I am younger than you
the reason you're able to exploit me now
is the same reason I continue:
I will be alive at your funeral
I will caress your folded fingers
softly break your stilled hands

## JOHN

He lives
in the tunnel of smoke
spiralling from his lips.
Sleepless nights
washing out caves beneath his eyes, knows that
there will be no light
shining at the end of the long nightmare.
Oh Vancouver
with your circus gaiety littering the horizon
with your skirtfuls of costume jewels
rambling into the ocean--
You have forgotten how to give!
Smoke dissipates around him like
ghosts without stories;
faces fall apart
blurring in his myopic vision.
The seat of his pants sags when he shuffles
threadbare
speaking of loss, an unforgiven past.  Yet
neither the Vancouver sea (nor its sky) will receive him . . .

The neons burn holes into the city's fabric
glaring at the man of the streets.

# TAMBOURINE MAN

He says "I love you"
four cylinders sprout from his palms.
This time, the pills are colors of spring--
pastel pink
orange sherbert
flaming in the light.
Their names have escaped me.

The waves crowd in
skinny and voracious
feeding upon the shore.
The ocean sloshes drunk
beneath a pale-bellied sky, threatening sickness.
His eyes are islands
the wrinkles at their corners
mapping foreign lands.

"You'll feel peaceful now" he smiles
with his desert eyes
"You'll feel warm inside"
and then it doesn't matter that it's hard work
forcing down the circles and ovals
into a rolling stomach

When he squints at the sea, the sailboats
ridden by men
clutching at wings of rainbows
I sneak eyes at the inside of his elbow
the swollen, black veins
marvelling that happiness can be injected

The diamond sun journeys across the sky
searing hollows into the sand.
I fly with it, and with this being
whose candy-colored kisses float me
above the shards of shells on the beach
high where sticky spiderwebs of light
caress me

# HOLES

you looked this morning into your net
I was entangled among your accomplishments
I flashed and spun and seemed willing
to ask the right questions
accept that you knew the answers

how many before me have tumbled
into your hole of need
the workaholic hours, the blinding drunks
this is not a style of living
where is the evidence of a life in light
except for the leather-bound photo album, holding together
famous people wearing bellbottoms
and tortured smiles

I could break your past like a brittle ornament
expect no pain this time
expect your father's face to crumple between your knees
sweating and lurching into his neck
your choking adolescent sobs to frighten him
that he will shed the military uniform
lick the blood slowly from your fingers
that he will leave you alone
this time

when I look up next
I will hear nothing but the hum of lights
see an empty bench behind the observation window
I will step off the high board
hands pointed to stab the water
welcome its emotionless depths

## THERE ONCE WAS A COMMUNE IN MY BACK YARD

a dove fluttered from the window
of the house across the alley.

the people inside
used to sprawl on the back porch sometimes
in summer:
a vision of legs and arms
long hair
love beads
and shirts studded with buttons I could never read
from where I was
watching them

they left one day

I knew
because the windows stared
gashes in a blank face;
a broken lamp teetered against
cardboard boxes piled high.

the landlord had come
and was pulling up the organic vegetables
hammering in a fence
sawing down branches of the apple tree

# MAMA'S BOY

Mama's little golden boy
came home today in funeral black
his hair a rainbow of false-bright colors
his rosy face a death-white mask

Mama sees her curlers reflected
in the hurting metal of his chains
She imagines herself impaled
on the wicked spears of his 10-inch spikes

Mama stands, hands outstretched
a timeless hourglass figure
facing her son's fiery gaze:
"My little boy, come back to me"

Mama's little golden boy
shining now from pins and studs
shrugs his shoulders and turns away
to the music of a dozen jangling bracelets

## AN AUTUMN PHOTOGRAPH

The camera stares on silver legs.
A woman leans into the wind
sweeping away sheafs of hair from her face
with icicle hands.
Leaves splotch blood onto the sidewalk
pooling at her feet.
Seagulls circle wide,
handkerchiefs flung weeping out of the wash,
wheeling around a mass of phosphorescent sun.
Water gurgles from the park fountain
stealing shards of sunshine
where she positions her foot like a stone cherub.

A man tiptoes quickly
from behind the mounted camera.
He slips his arm around the woman's waist.
They smile
and the glass eye winks in approval.

## EXPERIENCE AT THE BUS STOP

"hey, you got a smoke" the bum asks
poking about in the rain
so I give him the stub between my lips
offering ashes for the warmth he needs

he takes it and inhales hard
saying "what's life without a wife?
hey that rhymes; I could write me a poem"
but the poetry seemed to escape with his words

he shifts his cane to pat my arm
"well, I'd better be on my way
it's three miles walk to my welfare cheque"
and I see it is not a cane at all
but a discarded stick from some lumber yard

# FIRST EXPERIENCES

I entered my first pub at thirteen.
It was supposed to be a unique experience--
"something to tell your grandchildren about," the man insisted, his
moustache curling upwards when he smiled. Grandchildren?
Already assuming.

The men behind the counter, with their swarthy,
bare arms, flexed mermaids on their skin when they moved.
It was as though I'd walked into a preconception of something.

No one noticed as I slid into a booth.
On the screens there were men wrestling,
a football game--the images hard and masculine, bodies contacting
and colliding. Conversations mixed and flowed in currents through
the darkness. Light from the afternoon leaked inside, the color
of melted silver coins, in long stripes.

The man came over with beer, a liquid shifting inside sturdy
glasses. Can't remember much about him, either, except the small
things--how his glasses were the kind that darkened in sunlight and
became clear indoors, and that he was bald beneath his motorcycle
helmet.

The beer had a comfortable seeping warmth in my stomach, but
in my mouth the taste was unfamiliar, bordering on unpleasant. I
swallowed each gulp quickly, trying to get it inside
me before the taste could register on my tongue.

Afterwards the man and I went to a grocery store for mints, making
a show out of disguising the smell of booze on my breath.
The woman behind the counter smiled at us as though we were lovers.

# PROTEST

(huddling in the rain)

"the weather is bad but nothing can stop us now"
4. . .3. . .2. . .1. . .
and the missile takes off

speeding down its pathway in the sky

      a whistle of steel

      shooting
stars and stripes
      flapping in the wind

("Test the bomb!  On Reagan's lawn!"
dancing for preservation
   chanting to drown out the insanity)

"It's a success"
small men stand tall
guzzling champagne      patting each other on the back
straightening ties
the world is dismissed with a TV switch

("it's hard to hang on in zero degree weather"
the stench of wet cardboard signs
banners unfurling upside down)

"at this very moment, the missile has landed safely on its
first free-flight test"

(a fist connects)

*&*

## BUTTERFLY

FOR JULIE BELMAS, YOUNGEST OF THE VANCOUVER FIVE, APPEALING A
20-YEAR PRISON SENTENCE (BOMBING OF LITTON SYSTEMS FACTORY,
ROBBERY, FIRE-BOMBING OF RED HOT VIDEO)

Grappling with a language twisted in the hands of the law,
her fingers pull apart Kleenex like paper dolls.  The heads
of the judges preside over the courtroom where she stands.

A policeman searches in my bag for a gun? a knife? outside
the soundproof doors where she awaits judgment, the whirring fans
overhead dancing wings of light on steel bars.

(running on the white sands, miles of bones turned to dust,
turning more bones to dust.  Throwing the world off
these shoulders, away from this hourglass of death it spilled,
as seagulls scream and scatter . . .)

A politician swears in an elevator, then steps out into the
lobby to greet cameras, clean-shaven,
smiling.

The microphone extracts strands of speech from her history.
Fingers push at the prison doors, knowing they might open
only to greet a charred and disemboweled world.

A butterfly without the gift of speech, her white wings
flit over a heap of shredded Kleenex flowers

# RM. 809, DELTA PLACE

thought it would be a good place to hide, this hotel room
the sun's too bright today
he says the women eating lunch on the steps of Robson Square
give him an erection
their seething mass of bare arms and legs

you didn't know what to expect
a slick briefcase, an ordinary face
enhanced by the cut of his suit, a river of silk tie
recognition shivers through your body

he presses the room number into your hand
like a coin
he's got steel hair and an artist's nose
looks paranoically left and right as you walk down the street
together
instructs you to arrive separately
wouldn't want to be seen by his clientele
you sun yourself for precisely five minutes and follow

a "Please Do Not Disturb" sign is slung over the doorknob
like a scalp
it's stockings off and then everything
but first that magic obligation of money
crisp bills change hands, in this way
you touch him for the first time
you lift up your shirt
he devours you with copper-hard eyes
you do it on the bed
his hands are clean, the nails pink and perfect
scrubbed like a boy's
you see your own thighs like someone else's sculpture
you savour the firmness of the mattress
the Oriental sketching on the wall
the sight of a city magazine you once wrote for on the bedside table
seems like that was another person
the one you need to fuck away
the skin of his eyelids stretches taut
the bedspread is the color of bruises
you don't look at yourself, the thickness in his eyes
is no mirror

later, he adjusts his tie in the doorway
refuses to tell you his last name
composes his face for the next board meeting
frustrations unleashed
batteries replenished
you admire his suit covertly in the bathroom mirror
apply the lipstick he's licked off like candy
you want to shake hands afterwards
--a most agreeable business transaction--
but you've become a shameful thing
he regards you from a great distance behind his eyes
you pick up the city magazine
start to tell him about the career he's replaced
the suit is a thin shell over his impatience
he shows you to the door
like an editor with a deadline

## HANGING ON

I wait for you to emerge
hands outstretched
the bottle concealed against your anorexic body.
It's an acquired taste:
the methadone is Tang-flavored, bitter
brimming over the plastic measuring cup
otherworldly

We swallow
tongues lapping at the cup's bottom.
It pleases me to see your muddy eyes
pinpointed
no different from my own.
It pleases me to hear the sound of your laughter
tongue racing over teeth
and to recognize the echo.

It is unlikely now that the sun will wake
and stab me
immobile on the breast of my pillow.
Unlikely that it will condemn this body
buried beneath the covers:
muscles twitching and dancing,
heart struggling underwater.

Tonight, the Lions' Gate Bridge, the man-made web of glitter
arching, ripping into the sky
strung out
holds no attraction.
I have forgotten the need to be whipped
by the wind
to calculate the distance between bridge and ocean;
the need to drown in the dimming lights of our city.

Shoulders roped by red suspenders
snapping against his body,
he signals hello from across the room.
She plots diamond scissors separating elastic,
color bleeding through cotton.

She captures him, demanding hugs.
He holds her on sanded steps,
suspenders barring bodies.
A sharp flower of light
dies instantly in their faces

Later, the photograph will appear
in some arts magazine:
her head on his chest,
his face a mask of shock
as though tiny brushes had stroked the skin;
his eyes stretched circular,
convulsed by knives of light.

Unconscious under studio lamps,
her palms turn up in a gesture of appeal.
His muddy eyes stir, thicken.
She follows these pockets of reproach,
reads the writing on her wrists.

While chairs thrust scrawny limbs into the air,
the man bound up in red suspenders
dressed to complement shredded wrists,
cradles the poet in his arms
before the stampede

### BEHIND GLASS

Headlights twitch in the night,
curve white balls into the garden.
She steps off the balcony, nightgown
fleeing behind her,
breath blooming shapeless flowers

Light snares her, lifts her
onto a web of lines
arms of brightness suspend her
above the sweet pea garden of summer
beams and rulers crisscrossing
Her arms clamber, grasp ropes of light
stretch and weave

In her short gown she crawls
hand over hand across rods of light
over the children's sandbox
the corn exploding yellow hair
Her escape mapped across garden roof,
she tiptoes across a stray frisbee

(there must be arms that remember
nightgown and the shape beneath it
a mouth cut like a star
pressing over her own
hands will travel her like light)

Escaping above garbage cans silver as knight's armor
the dog and the scarecrow bum in the garden--
Through the curtain's parted lips
the mouth of night swallows car headlights

## CONCLUSION

She likes it cold here--
her hands, scorched by his heat,
dance backwards to safety.
Shot by arrows of exhaustion,
his eyes pulse blue hearts, his temples
swell in tenderness,
but she seeks no refuge in soft spots,
trains instead on the cutting edges.

She remembers now the why:
the years have knit the nerves in her shoulders
high into her neck,
snapped muscles locked and secret.
Voices like warm taffy
trussed her in ropes of platitudes
while armies waited to spring unsheathed,
eyes crossed in disdain.
The hungry ones wait still
for her moment of ripeness--
they will sate their appetites
on her moment of quick weakening.

His fingers spread smooth tendrils across her skin.
Furrows cemented between her eyes,
she stacks the barriers between them
--such a small space to fill--
plucks his hairs from the mattress,
draws bitterness tight around her body.
She stands him outside, and his brave smile
shrivels in the winter frost.

## TWO SMOKERS

Their fingers meet to pass a lighter.
She flicks it once, twice,
flame leaps into faces.

"Pyromaniacs are sexually frustrated," he teases
but she shakes her head,
grinds roller against flint,
watches fire prance.
Her eyes ache from holding his,
thick with smoke reflections.

In bed, she lies awake with a firefly
between her nails,
watches ashes dive to carpet,
twists to inspect the burns.
Groaning, he speaks through strata of sleep:
"Please don't move.
I need you.
Hold me"
then gropes at the wall,
finds flesh in his dreams,
murmurs  content.

She stubs out her cigarette,
scattering sparks--
She watches the trail of smoke
drift towards the ceiling,
hesitate, fall apart.

# FREEBASING

fingers urgent against the window.  three a.m.

you fall indoors
a bubble clutched in shivering hands.
wind sweeps you into lamplight;  a carpet
floats you towards kitchen chair.

fingers frantic
you seduce mad light into this contraption:
bottle and pipe
starred with white grains like fleas
hopping away from skeletal hands

your eyes gouged, sleepless
the pipe wobbles on your palm
like breast of bird fluttering in hand
milk-pale
cocaine crystals blooming in a glass globe

flame shoots into pipe
smoke swirls inside the bottle
a chemical smell here--
your mouth gasps for this strange bird
sucks and swallows

black figure blazes

the bottle clears
a trace of smoke escapes bleached lips
your grin wraps rubbery
around the splintering room

*EL*

## CANADIAN BROADCASTING CORPORATION

### TELEVISION WRITERS' WORKSHOP, 1989

I

It's no use:
never anything here but disposable lines, long discarded,
only to be yearned after later
like names like voices like the unmistakeable face

He pinches up the still-burning filter, its offensive discharge,
crushes sparks into ashes.
Smoke curls around eyes
watchful in that windowless room;
prints on walls I squint at with birds' feet between my brows
to avoid the dull humming in my brain

His eyes skip amused down the table,
cleverly circle notebooks and scripts to search
the faces bleached of expression.
He can only say "It has taken time" from the safe distance of recovery

II

They tell me this editor never forgot her past
just doesn't talk about it in these inappropriate rooms.
It's been misplaced in files, unsolicited correspondence,
locked away behind windows without latches, restraining her
like a suicidal stockbroker.

She wears deliberate rose shades and it is then,
juggling them careful on the steps outside,
gripping ears and nose,
that I see the city through her eyes:
the smack of purple sky
reeling my brain back into the lobby,
the flash and retreat of buildings arranged
by comic-book law

I see that when she moves off solitary
from the closed room, the hurting light,
she wishes to stand alone on pink concrete
to blink the veins from her eyes and watch them wing off
in scarlet lightning

III

The editors' eyes will forever run
blue lakes down the conference table.
The tired hair they tear and wipe
from their heads in handfuls
reflects in the unblinking rows of stone faces.

I never catch the hardness till it's too late:
till its legs are crossed and
it is smoking a cigarette--
till the slow eyes surround me, bodies they belong to
fading into chairs and couches.
It leaps at me like the pink and purple slices
of sky and concrete and glass:
the bridge of a nose stiffened, knocked into place,
the cheekbones rebelling east and west,
that twist of lips. Mistaking the analytical glare
for kind brown eyes.

Smoke dwindles around us:
the sexy slow-motion falling
of a net over naked limbs.

LSD, ETC.


Someone's finger etches a heart on your back
but you're asleep
your finger won't return the message.
It's curled up into your hand
a white spider snuggled against webs of hair.

Morning already,
another square on the calendar.
I dare not urge the curtains aside
to confront the sky--
I'd rather keep watch over that spider
content in its home.

Your pills are rumbling in me again
trapped
unwilling to dissolve, to stroke
my corpse's lids downwards
onto drowsy cheeks.

It's the blotter that's propping my eyes open.
You plucked up that fat purple flower
and laid it on my tongue
enslaving me to its petals
blooming through my bloodstream.

We pointed at the dough-faced passerby
"Unenlightened", we whispered, smug
our words exchanging lips.
We reduced them to burping toads,
whores cupping silicone breasts--
whatever we wanted.

There were colors, then crawlings.
The city was scraped away by a sidewalk
infested with pink insects,
studded with cheap glitter.
Even the veins on your face crawled
protruding
but I fingered them anyway
seeking secrets I could reveal,
then steal

Fool!
You left your pharmacy on the bathroom counter.
Didn't you dream that one night I might tiptoe
away from the critical dawn
and slide some 'ludes down my throat?
Didn't you dream that one night I might hurry
Darvon, Valium, rainbows of pills
into the leather pouch you tossed in my direction once?

But my eyelids should shut like coffins soon.
Stars should burst out of the make-believe night
Soon.

Someone's finger etches a heart on your back
but you're asleep,
your finger won't return the message.

# WHAT WE DO IN THE NAME OF MONEY

heavy feet on the back stairs announce
300 lbs. of stock promoter
you wonder what it's like to drive across town at midnight
for a blow job
guess it's no different than going out for a hamburger

every time you see a father now
in real life or on TV
you see you're young enough to be their daughter
instead you've become the girl they visit
on nights like these
you caress their faces differently
than a daughter's hands
it changes the way you watch happy families in the sitcoms

tug the sash of your silk robe tighter
walk fast to the door
his mouth opens as if to swallow you
like the boxes of shortbread cookies he consumes
in his unconfessed loneliness
you know him well, 2 years and enough conversations
but tonight the history doesn't show
you light his cigarettes, put on coffee
exaggerate the slavery he hands you with the folded bills

the robe falls like water down a rock
he sprawls on your bed
the fan in the bathroom whirs for the next hour
the apartment lights burn your brain into white metal
your thighs straddle his shoulders like run-on sentences
his hands clench the edges of the comforter
brown and defenseless
he raises them to cover his face
his mindless words are lost to you, the expletives
forced out between lubricated lips
your bed is awash with his sweat
you will wrap yourself in its smell for days
its acridity relieved by cologne

memo:   don't brush your teeth for 15 minutes afterwards
when you should be licking your lips
he watches you now with that cool reservation
only guilt can bring
on the slow painful descent down the back stairs
he puckers his lips
whistles at the sightless constellations.

## SURFACES

Hanging
an enigma of human flesh
from the edges of the sky:
groping for a fingernail of sanity
I compose a mask over the gargoyle
even as the pavement disembowels me
and my hands bleed sunsets for someone's amusement.

## MIDNIGHT

the cry of the phone heralds
another drunken editor
the night splits down its centre
fog brings memories of knives and long walks taken
down the middle lane of the road
it is midnight and the light they capture you by
blinds the cameras in the room
somewhere people are breathing
they cough, reach for another cigarette
strain eyes at computer screens
follow the dense lines on a page
lie down beside imaginary bodies in bed
somewhere someone is laughing

I see you have come to warm me with your eager ghosts
your effeminate hands
the moon is never quite Lawrencian
the backdrop never fits the scene you wish to create
with your new leather coat and clean shirt
I smile anyway at the gesture
the night implodes with color
the sky exhales
its breath is tawny and glowing
this hour is not safe
it slices like a guillotine
midnight is a soft throat you fumble for
it is a beginning and an end
it begs apologies and promises
you make both, profuse with wine
you must steal this moment
before the collective unconscious wakes

the fog congregates in banks along the hill
it's an upward climb to your house
you don't know if the car will make it this time
you gather the fog in your hands, press it to your face
be grateful that tonight, you draw no blood
evoke nothing but the threat of a hangover
the couch is conveniently next to the proud bottle
your favorite nostalgic tunes play
midnight releases a smell not unlike hurt blossoms
you imbibe your own solitude
drink it down to the dregs
there are no messages for you to unfurl
no fortunes to hang these minutes on
you've paid your dues, and now a stranger turns up
to collect your reward

## FLYING HOME

it takes time to get re-acquainted
it's not til the last day that comfort begins to settle
like that ratty crocheted spread
on your armchair

I squeeze my eyes shut
on this final connecting flight
wring out exhaustion like dirty water
from a tubful of clothes
drink wine with Canadian passengers

the written word is so excruciatingly
different from the ones we speak
I blame our silence on sleeplessness
we who are used to elaborate letters
the rare misleading photograph

I have not changed, I mouth silently
at the bathroom mirror's appliqued butterflies
I wipe off lipstick and eyeliner
strip myself barren as the trees
we passed on the highway across the border

when you ran for the rest stop bathroom
I wrote "Love is an eight-hour drive
through rain and fog" in my notebook
I faced your eyes and blinked
at their bottled timidity

you have navy pupils and green irises
I pick at a chipped fingernail
refrain from using the word "beautiful"
the executives in the airport eye
your salvaged clothes
your broken jeans

it's not til afterwards I remember
how to phrase the perfect apology
how to spend time with you over breakfast
how to leave properly
we are after all so silent as people
so wordless

we'll still send letters, of course
conceal our growing differences
your hug at the terminal smells of sweaty shyness
flying home, the advertised golden horizon
diminishes with the distance
into a lightless night

## LETTER TO THE EDITOR

the lines of the aquarium crisscross
a whale slides and screams behind the glass
some say the pool's dirty, point at brown flecks and scum
I press my face up against the trapped water
see a slick slow body, a giant decision to birth

pills dampen my tongue in the bathroom mirror
ease open the gate of my throat
they don't stop the heartbeats though
like a dozen roses in my chest
I need someone to recite the four stages of recovery
acceptance hides behind that corner in a black hat

if my eyes had brimmed over
your office would have become an aquarium
I would have leapt down your lazy mouth like a fish
made sure it was truth gleaming in those eyes
not another tired insincerity
I would have breathed out a necklace of bubbles
danced my arms into ridiculous fins
shouted silently:
"Two months' rent
the most ingenious revenge
a cover page in my portfolio--all lost"
while you looked on alarmed
clutching drenched files to your chest

I would spit ice cubes then and show you the special trick I have
of numbing the lick of razor blades
I'd open my freezer door, where packages of frozen shrimp
and wide-eyed squid
nudge the bloodstains of cut wrists stuck to ice
I'd convince you that pain is an expensive sensation
and a privilege
I'd clasp child's arms around your slippery body
ride you to the surface of the pool
somehow, the check would not have gotten wet
you'd slip it into my mouth
like a lover's tongue

## I AM SURE THIS IS

better in the long run
this mixture of white wine and bile in the bathroom sink
like something marinated in a musty fridge
you haven't gotten old enough nor rich enough in the past year
for someone like me to want you
muscles and tight jeans notwithstanding
that familiar hurt look and all the while I'm thinking
of someone else, clean businessman hands
another touch, you could say it was like death
peculiar but awesome
I followed its patchouli scent

drunk now as a forgotten poet in a once-popular bar
eager to sell or sacrifice any part of himself
for that starry career
scotches and slowly sipped tomato beers
those desperate kisses at the bus station
I remember simply an evening where it rained
after he left, I wore high heels and it seemed
I had miles to walk alone
downhill

I'm willing to go anywhere but here
someplace sandy, with highways and many cars
I shall wear durable clothing
give up the struggle and start new
someplace cleansed of old miseries
shamefully remembered bodies
for now my eyes are so heavy
I blame it on the wind that blew up from the beach
blew the shoreline into my eyes
I pump bravely at tears but none arrive
not even four a.m. when no one hears them

you never cried either, at least not in my company
I wanted to see you broken
wanted it to be me who'd worked you over
till everything crashed inside you
like one prolonged orgasm
your adventurous hands do nothing for me
I've experienced the skill of numerous tongues
all the orifices partaken of
I've nothing special here to give you
nothing that can't be bought, and
most men could outbid you any day

certainly you have no success, just a pair of hands and needle marks
in your arms
a grinding crotch and those punk boots
I've made it so far without needing that
lived through the losses of others
the fights and their moves to different cities
I assure you
there's no bridging ground
maybe we'll meet and have coffee someday
for now, I am sure this is best

## POETIC MANOEUVRES

you are not who you claim, not
what the telephone voice implies
there were dozen of corners to choose from
for this rendezvous
instead, the colors of the day fade upon the downtown square
harbinger of sad endings and disasters
the arms of the clock point back to other hours
fraught meetings on wooden benches
secrets tearing at the seams of silence
I cross the street with a departure already in hand
the accidental brush of our bodies shows that no part of me
fits snugly into you

your practiced poet's poses amaze me:
hand on chin
head cocked
eyes gazing soulfully out the window
as a photographer I would capture you on film
submit the arrogance of your face
the aging effects of booze and cigarettes and of course words
have ignored you in passing
you claim to read my thoughts
do you not suppose I could think lies
that I could will lies like bright butterflies into my brain
this is one conquest I'll never allow
impeccable in my definitions, I scorn your use of the word 'love'
an euphemism for crueler truths

the pull of your hands propels me forward for
a sharp bite on the neck
your laughter, difficult to gauge
shakes like a rattle in your stomach
it bursts from my lungs
our silver table tilts towards morning
alcohol electricity worn off
the light in your eyes difficult to see by
the rape of your tongue reminds me of other
unwanted tongues, multiplying hands
you have no mystery I must plunder
your body quivers readily with lies
arrows you line up to aim
there is nothing original to be found in seduction
every word is doomed to be a cliché, at the very least
a repetition

I would like to apologize for us both
and the lonely bald man behind you in the bar
and the woman in the backless dress who teased him
anorexic lines parenthesizing her smile:
yes
the girl swimming laps in the pool outside the window
has drowned, the water lies flat and blue as boredom
you can't begin to imagine my powerful dismay
at your arm around my waist
your mouth pinpointing mine
the street at dawn is a splintered shade of grey
a forlorn taxi speeds away
in the rearview mirror, I see the lights of the city dim
beside your beautiful pathos

# Acknowledgments

I would like to thank the following people, each of whom contributed to the realization of this book:

- Robert Best, my first mentor, who demanded perfection;
- Sue Nevill, for showing me I had enough poems for a collection;
- Crawford Kilian, for reading and listening;
- David McFadden, who got me away from the typewriter long enough to compile and submit this collection;
- *The Province* newspaper, especially Patricia Graham, for being a source of support and encouragement in my career

-- *E.L.*

## About the Poet

Evelyn Lau has been publishing poetry and prose since she was thirteen. Now eighteen, she has had her poetry appear in *Prism International, The New Quarterly, Queen's Quarterly* and *Canadian Author and Bookman,* among other literary magazines. Her prose has been published in *MacLean's, Vancouver Magazine* and *The Antigonish Review.* And she has won six awards for her poetry.

For two years, Evelyn lived on "the streets" in a world of drugs and prostitution recording these experiences in a journal. She left the streets in 1988 at the age of seventeen and extracts from this journal became the best-selling *Runaway: Diary of a Street Kid,* which stayed on bestseller lists across Canada for months.

Evelyn is now a freelance writer for the *Province* and the *Globe & Mail* as well as working on a collection of short stories. She lives in Vancouver.